# Favorite
# CLASSICAL Melodies

## CLARINET

Arranged and Recorded by David Pearl
("Brandenburg Concerto No. 5, First Movement" arranged and recorded by Donald Sosin)

Cherry Lane Music Company
Director of Publications/Project Supervisor: Mark Phillips

ISBN: 978-1-60378-408-5

*Visit our website at www.cherrylaneprint.com*

T0069318

# CONTENTS

# AVE MARIA

CLARINET

By Charles Gounod and Johann Sebastian Bach

**Moderately slow**

# BRANDENBURG CONCERTO NO. 5,
# FIRST MOVEMENT

By Johann Sebastian Bach

CLARINET

# CARO MIO BEN

CLARINET

By Giuseppe Giordani

**Moderately slow**

# CLAIR DE LUNE

CLARINET

By Claude Debussy

# FUNERAL MARCH OF A MARIONETTE

CLARINET

by Charles Gounod

**Moderately fast, in 2**

# GYMNOPÉDIE NO. 1

CLARINET

By Erik Satie

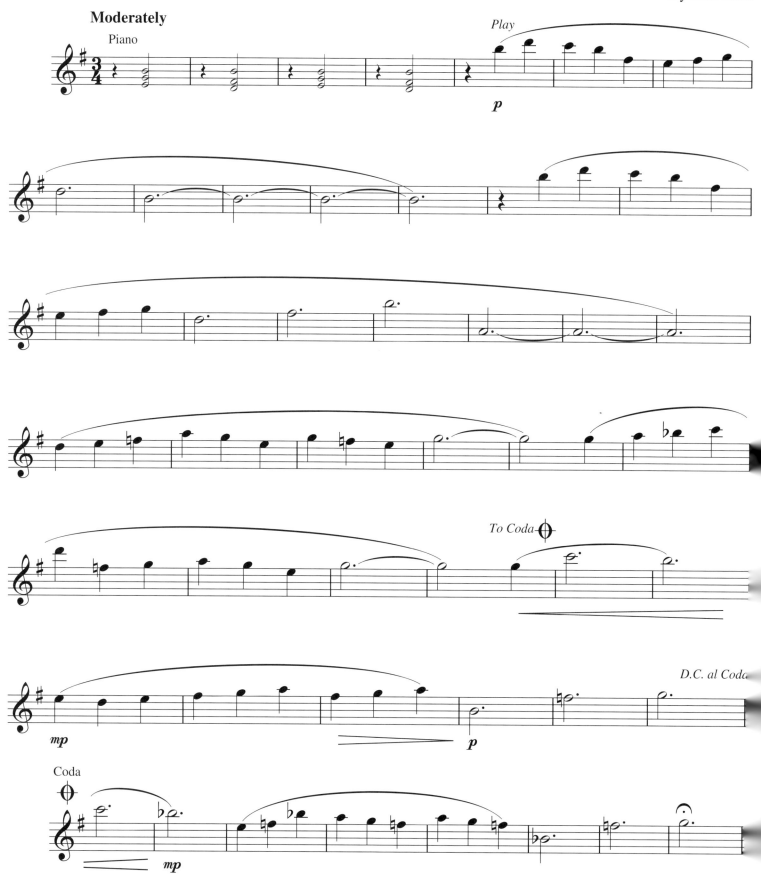

# HALLELUJAH CHORUS

from *Messiah*

**CLARINET**

By George Frideric Handel

# HUNGARIAN DANCE NO. 5

CLARINET

By Johannes Brahms

**Moderately**

**Slower**

**Tempo I**

# MINUET
## (from String Quintet in E Major)

By Luigi Boccherini

**CLARINET**

**Moderately**

# PIANO SONATA NO. 14 "MOONLIGHT"

## First Movement

CLARINET

By Ludwig van Beethoven

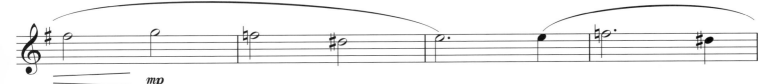

# SYMPHONY NO. 5

### First Movement

By Ludwig van Beethoven

**CLARINET**

**Moderately fast**

# WILLIAM TELL OVERTURE

CLARINET

By Gioacchino Rossini

**Moderately fast**

# POMP AND CIRCUMSTANCE

TRACK 13

CLARINET

By Edward Elgar